The Worshipful Company of

DISTILLERS

A Short History

Michael Berlin

Phillimore

Founder of the Company – 1638
SIR THEODORE TURQUET DE MAYERNE (1573-1655)
(Photograph courtesy of the Assistant Librarian, Royal College of Physicians)

The Worshipful Company of
DISTILLERS

A Short History

1996

Published by
PHILLIMORE & CO. LTD.
Shopwyke Manor Barn, Chichester, West Sussex

ISBN 1 86077 030 4

Printed and bound in Great Britain by
LAWRENCE-ALLEN LTD.
Weston-super-Mare, Avon

Contents

List of Illustrations

Author's Preface

There is no need to justify the writing of the history of an institution which is more than three hundred years old but a 'short history' which dates back to the early 17th century needs some slight explanation. This work is intended as an abridgement of a long and fascinating story. It is hoped that it will serve as a invitation to others to further research, rather than as a definitive history. For purposes of brevity the usual scholarly apparatus has been omitted but some indication of the source of quotations is provided in the text. The main source for this work is the Court Minute Books of the Distillers, on deposit along with the rest of the Company's records at Guildhall Library. The account of the formation of the Company is largely based on the State Papers, Domestic series for the reign of Charles I at the Public Record Office. A brief guide to further reading is provided at the end. The author wishes to thank members of the Distillers' Company, especially Past Masters Mr. Nigel Strofton, Mr. Michael Druitt and Court Assistant Mr. Nigel Churton, for their advice and encouragement, and the staff of the Guildhall Library, especially Mr. Andrew Riley and Mr. Stephen Freeth, for their unflagging assistance and support.

Introduction:
London in the Early 17th Century

The creation of the Distillers' Company in 1638 occurred at time of change and upheaval in the history of London. The ancient City of London, and the adjoining City of Westminster were being slowly transformed by population growth, economic expansion and social change. As the population of the city expanded from roughly 50,000 inhabitants in 1550 to 250,000 in the late 1630s, the built-up area of the metropolis stretched outward from the straggling suburbs around the medieval walls. To the east, north and west, open fields were fast giving way to new suburbs.

The City of London was the teeming commercial and financial heart of the ancient metropolis, with markets for all manner of goods and services, from butchers' and fishmongers' stalls in the open markets, to the merchants' counting houses and goldsmith bankers of Lombard Street. Presiding over the City were the Lord Mayor, Sheriffs and Court of Aldermen, who governed in combination with the civic assemblies known as the Common Council and Common Hall. The working life of the City was regulated by them in conjunction with the hundred-odd guilds or livery companies. These were associations of merchants, artisans and traders who oversaw the production and marketing of goods, participated in civic elections, raised the City's militias or trained bands, distributed alms for the poor and took part in the elaborate pageantry that marked City life. The tremendous wealth of the City of London was a handsome prize to the eyes of a greedy courtier and a necessitous monarch.

The foundation of the Distillers' Company occurred on the eve of a political crisis between the monarchy and Parliament that was to lead to the upheavals of the Civil War. It was to be a conflict in which the City of London and the livery companies were to play a central rôle. In the run-up to the Civil War relations between the Stuart monarchy and the City of London were strained to breaking point as the Crown strove to tap the City's wealth in a variety of ways. The City Corporation and the livery companies were pressured to allow Court favourites to enjoy monopolistic privileges in trade and industry.

The Early History of Distilling

Distillation is an ancient art which involves the conversion of various substances into vapours by means of heat and of condensing these vapours into liquid form. The history of the art of distilling long predates the creation of a commercial distilling industry and of the Distillers' Company. The art of distilling is as old as recorded history and finding a particular point of origin is as difficult as finding the fount of recorded human knowledge. Cultures as diverse as ancient China and ancient Africa were fully versed in the basic techniques of distillation of various non-alcoholic substances used as medicines, perfumes, dyes and foodstuffs. The most important centre for distilling in classical antiquity was Alexandria, renowned throughout the ancient world as a place of learning and experimentation. From Alexandria knowledge of the techniques of distilling and various other related chemical processes were diffused to other sites.

During the fourth century A.D. the Alexandrian chemists, many fleeing religious persecution, migrated to the relative tolerance of Persia, taking with them their skills. Here techniques and skills were finely honed. The spread of Islam throughout the eastern and western Mediterranean, including Spain, in the eighth century was of profound importance in the dispersal of this ancient legacy. As with so many other new techniques, the Arab presence in the Iberian peninsula introduced the art of distillation into western Europe and in the process new discoveries and techniques were perfected. From Spain, the Arabic versions of the ancient techniques were transferred to Italy, where the process of alcohol distillation was discovered, probably by alchemists at the famous medical school at Salerno, some time in the early 12th century. From Italy the art of distilling was diffused to France and Germany, the new skills transported by the migration of Italian apothecaries. Their products were various distillations of the by-products of wine which came to be known as 'strong waters' and 'burnt wines' (or *brand wein, brandewijn*, hence the English 'brandy wine' or brandy). The outbreak of bubonic plague in 1348 and subsequent epidemics helped to spread demand for the distilled waters. Doctors prescribed these 'burnt wines' and 'waters' in the belief that they inhibited disease. Aqua vitae, literally 'the water of life', one of the main products of the early commercial distillers, was valued because it was thought that it prolonged life.

But the process of change was slow. Some time at the end of the 14th century the process of distilling corn spirit was discovered. The new techniques were often kept as secrets among their practitioners, and confined largely to Italy, Germany and France. It is not known when distilling was first practised in Britain. Distilling in Scotland is said to date from the late 15th century and the Irish distillery is said to have had a similar venerable lineage. It seems that such distilling as took place in England in this period was largely confined to monasteries and to private houses. It is traditionally thought that the dissolution of the monasteries by Henry VIII dispersed the store of skills retained in these institutions as the former inmates turned to commercial distilling. Much distilling of non-alcoholic 'simple waters', distillations of flowers, herbs and plants was undertaken by women in country households. Domestic distilling was to remain important despite the growth of a commercial industry.

By the late 16th century a commercial industry was beginning to develop in continental Europe. In the Low Countries distilling was perfected to a high art. A distillate of alcohol using juniper berries was reputedly invented by the chemist of Leiden, Franciscus Sylvius, for medicinal purposes.

Distilling in the 17th
century, from John French,
The Art of Distillation,
1667 (Guildhall Library,
Corporation of London)

Commercial distilling took place at Amsterdam, Dordrecht, Leiden, Brille, Haarlem, Delft and Alkmaar. As the industry grew, guilds of distillers began to be formed in these towns. The first taste for the 'strong waters' of the Continent was said to have been brought to England by English soldiers who had fought with the Dutch against the Spanish in the 1570s. Whatever the source of this new-found habit, domestic demand for aqua vitae and other spirits grew in the later part of the reign of Queen Elizabeth I. Much of the demand for these products was for medicinal purposes but, on the long deep-sea voyages of the period, distilled spirits were discovered to last much longer than beer or ale, and as overseas trade expanded so too did demand for the distillers' products. Another product which the distillers provided was various forms of vinegar, known as alegar and beeregar and made from the by-products of the brewers.

In London this part of the distillers' art was said to have been introduced by Dutch and Flemish refugees who settled in the metropolis after the conflicts of the 1560s. By the end of Elizabeth's reign commercial distilling of both vinegar and spirituous liquors had grown to such an extent that it attracted the attention of Lord Burghley, chief minister to Queen Elizabeth I, who ordered an investigation of the trade. Reports told of the need to reform abuses, such as the use of corrupt ingredients and 'unwholesome stuff', and of the great difficulties in regulation, due to the fact that 'the trade doth concern so many poor men's livings'. As with so many other expanding areas of production the increasingly lucrative distilling trade attracted the interest of a patentee who sought a state-sanctioned monopoly over production. In 1594 a monopoly patent was granted by the Crown to Richard Drake to make aqua vitae, aqua composita and vinegar. This patent provoked great hostility from the 'poor men in the trade' and this revulsion against monopolies was manifested in the Parliament of 1601 which quashed Drake's patent along with a host of similar grants to patentees.

The Quest for Incorporation

Despite Parliament's distaste for such privileges James I and Charles I continued the policy of granting monopolies to courtly patentees. These monopolies often took the form of new incorporations of livery companies, vesting control of the trade in associations of craftsmen formed through the influence of a patentee. These new incorporations sometimes represented a direct challenge to the privileges of an existing livery company. Anyone with enough sway at Court was capable of securing royal approval for the grant of a charter of incorporation or patent that conferred legal powers to oversee and regulate branches of trade and industry. In the 1620s and 1630s monopoly rights were conferred by the Crown to groups and individuals dealing with virtually every imaginable product or commodity. Monopolies were created in the manufacture of playing cards, sewing pins, dice, soap, carriage springs and sweet wines. Frustration at the interference of the Court in the City's affairs led to the firm support shown by the citizens of the metropolis for Parliament's cause when the Civil War commenced. The foundation of the Distillers was part of the royal policy of encouraging monopolies that was so to antagonise City and parliamentary opinion.

The first recorded attempt to incorporate the distilling trade predates the foundation of the Distillers' Company by some seventeen years. A proposed 'Act for the relief of distillers and sellers of Aqua Vitae, Aqua Composita and other strong and hot waters in London and Westminster' was presented by the metropolitan distillers in the form of a petition to the Parliament of 1621. But the overall mood of the House of Commons was virulently against monopolies and the attempt at incorporation foundered. The failed distillers' petition is important because of the light it sheds on the state of the trade in the early 17th century. A commercial industry had developed servicing both metropolitan demand 'for those that be aged and weak in time of sudden qualms and pangs, and to help their old and decayed stomachs' but also supplying drink for the King's ships and merchant ships 'for use shipboard and for sale to foreign nations…by way of merchandise to the advancement of His Majesty's Customs and to the great and public profit and benefit of this realm'. The petition stated that the metropolitan industry supported 'two hundred families at the least within the cities of London and Westminster and the suburbs thereof using and exercising the said trade and bringing up many apprentices without employing them in any other service…'. Though the petition failed, the momentum for incorporation gathered apace. But it was not in Parliament that the distillers were to find solace but through the intervention of a group of influential members of the College of Physicians and intimates of Charles I.

The Founders of the Company: de Mayerne, Cademan and Brouncker

S ir Theodore Turquet de Mayerne (1573-1655), Baron de Aubonne was one of the foremost physicians of the early 17th century. Born at Mayerne near the Calvinist stronghold of Geneva, de Mayerne was the son of prominent French Protestant exiles Louis Turquet and Louise le Maçon who fled France in 1576 after the St Bartholomew's Eve massacre of the Huguenots at Paris. The closeness of his family to the Calvinist cause is attested to by his parent's choice of godfather, the eminent Genevan teacher and theologian, Theodore Beza. He was educated at Geneva, Heidelberg and the famous medical school at Montpellier from where he graduated as Doctor of Medicine in 1597. Deeply influenced by the new ideas of the Renaissance physician-cum-alchemist Paracelsus, de Mayerne achieved notoriety for publicly championing chemical remedies derived from Paracelsus in a series of public lectures and pamphlets. He is credited with the introduction of calomel into medical practice. Chemical medicine, which advocated the use of various synthetic compounds in the treatment of illness, was a hotly-disputed subject within the medical profession. Though condemned by the College of Physicians of the University of Paris, he found favour at the Court of King Henry IV.

He left Paris for London after helping to cure a visiting English peer who introduced him into the Court of James I. De Mayerne was granted an M.D. by Oxford University in 1606. Thereafter he went back to Paris but was recalled to England in 1611 at the direct request of James I who appointed him as First Physician. As First Physician he treated the immediate family and entourage of James I, delivering all of Queen Anne's six children, including the heir to the throne Prince Henry and his younger brother Prince Charles. James I conferred a knighthood on him in July 1624. His service at Court continued during the reign of Charles I. He later served as first physician to Charles' consort Henrietta Maria, an irony considering the Queen's acknowledged Catholicism. Admitted to the College of Physicians of London in 1616 he soon became one its most prominent fellows. De Mayerne was influential in disseminating some of the new Paracelsian

IMMEDIATE PAST MASTER'S BADGE
AND REVERSE

showing our founder, Sir Theodore de Mayerne

This badge was lost in the early 1980s. A new badge was presented by Past Master Walter Sichel in 1984. Subsequently this badge was found and the Court at that time decided to have an Immediate Past Master's Badge.

THE MASTER'S BADGE

Presented to the Company in 1984 by Walter Sichel
Master 1980-1981

'THE MISTRESS'S BADGE'
(The Master's Lady)

Presented to the Company by Norman Burrough, CBE
Master 1988-1989

Subsequently a safety chain was added by Mrs. Michael Broadbent

ideas into English medical practice and he engaged in chemical and physical experiments of the most diverse kinds. Though his main interest lay in the application of chemical experiment to medicine, his interests ranged from experimentation with new medical compounds to the making of enamels and the compilation of a cookery book consisting of elaborate English and French recipes. His medical status was such that he was invited to write the dedicatory preface to the first *Pharmacopoeia Londiniensis*, the first official chemical formula book for use by the Apothecaries' Company. De Mayerne's familiarity with the Stuarts and his interest in all branches of chemistry possibly accounts for his important rôle as the patron of the London Distillers.

The other two founders of the Distillers also had influence at the Stuart Court, using this favour to push for the incorporation of the Distillers' Company. Sir Thomas Cademan (?1590-1651) was a native of Norfolk and, in contrast to de Mayerne, a Catholic recusant. Educated at Cambridge and Padua, his Catholicism delayed his acceptance into the medical profession. Henrietta Maria's sympathies may have led him to being appointed Physician in Ordinary to the Queen in 1626. From that point onwards he became a prominent figure at Court. In addition to treating the Queen, Cademan was engaged in commercial distilling in partnership with another of the prime movers in the foundation of the Company, the courtier Sir William Brouncker (1585-1646). Brouncker was of a family of Wiltshire gentry who took possession of lands in Ireland during the Elizabethan period. Brouncker became a gentleman of the Privy Chamber in the Court of Charles I. The two men are described as joint holders of a patent for 'stilling and brewing' which they exercised from a house described as on the backside of St James' Park.

At some stage in the mid-1630s de Mayerne joined forces with Cademan and Brouncker in experimentation and in active pursuit of a monopoly patent for distilling. On 25 March 1636 de Mayerne and Cademan were granted for a yearly rent of £10 payable to the King, a 14-year patent for distilling strong waters and vinegar 'from perry and cider, etc.'. The patent was granted in recognition of their 'skill and great industry, after many chargeable experiments'. The same year a separate patent was granted to Brouncker which gave him licence to use a new method of improving the yields from distilled malt liquors. It is unclear who was responsible for these innovations. Cademan and Brouncker employed two men, named in a related petition to the Crown as Edward Bond and Michael Arnold, who may have actually carried out the new methods.

The three courtly patentees made common cause with the more numerous commercial distillers in pursuit of a charter of incorporation. Up to this point the practising commercial distillers were members of other livery companies such as the Grocers, Vintners and Brewers. Distilling was also extensively carried out by the Apothecaries who, prior to their incorporation in 1618 as the Society of Apothecaries, had been members of and subordinate to the government of the powerful Grocers' Company. The Apothecaries broke away from the Grocers' Company with the support of the Royal College of Physicians, including de Mayerne, who had lobbied for their separate incorporation. During the 1620s and 1630s the patronage of the College of Physicians was withdrawn as the two bodies fell into dispute about the alleged encroachment of the Apothecaries into areas deemed to be under the purview of the College. The attitude of the Apothecaries, themselves a break-away from another livery company, was to be a thorn in the side of the founders of the Distillers.

The Charter of Incorporation and the Coat of Arms

On 20 March 1638 de Mayerne, Brouncker and Cademan, together with some 99 distillers of 'spirits, aqua vitae, strong waters, vinegar and beeregar' within London and Westminster 'and 21 miles about', presented a joint petition for incorporation to King Charles. The campaign for incorporation culminated on 9 August 1638 when a charter of incorporation was formally granted by Charles I. This grant recognised the distillers as 'a body politic' to be thenceforth known by the name of the 'master, wardens, assistants and commonalty of Distillers of London'. The charter of incorporation is a lengthy document which laid out in 36 detailed clauses the internal government of the Company and the extent of its powers to regulate the trade. The purposes behind the grant are stated in the initial clauses. The regulation of the industry was justified as being:

> to the benefit of our people as well by the use and expense thereof within our kingdom and dominions as for victualling and furnishing our ships for and in long voyages and for our plantations and colonies in foreign parts and otherwise in the way of merchandise in sundry parts beyond the seas

The constitution of the Company resembled those of the other, older guilds and livery companies. The Company was to be governed by a master, three wardens and a 20-man Court of Assistants. Clauses in the charter named Cademan as the first master, and Sir William Brouncker, Thomas Dallock and Edward Booker as wardens and some 20 others, including de Mayerne, as assistants. De Mayerne was referred to by the honorific title of 'Founder of the Company'. The master and wardens were to be elected by seniority from amongst the Court of Assistants on a yearly basis on the first Tuesday after the Feast of St James the Apostle (25 July).* The charter empowered the Company to hold regular meetings at a hall or other premises, to own and assign lands, to use a common seal, to resort to courts of law and to administer oaths and enrol new members

---

* A later charter of 1687 specifies the election to take place on the Tuesday before the feast of St Matthew the Apostle.

WORSHIPFUL COMPANY OF DISTILLERS

Charter of Incorporation granted to the Company
by Charles I.

9 August 1638

as freemen. Membership in the Company was attained in one of three ways: apprenticeship (a period of service and training under the direct supervision of a member of the Company), patrimony (entry to the freedom of the Company through right of inheritance through the father, obtainable on payment of a fee), and redemption (membership granted in return for a payment to the Company at the discretion of the Court of Assistants). The task of enrolling new members was supervised by the Clerk, who was named in the charter as John Carwytham. An important clause specified that only those 'trained up and well experienced in the said art and mistery' were to be eligible for membership of the court of the Company. This clause perhaps in part helps to explain the long and close connection between the Company and the distilling industry, a tradition that was to be renewed in successive generations.

Control of the trade was the central purpose of the charter. Clauses in the charter gave the Company extensive powers to oversee the practice of distilling in all its forms. The Company was vested with powers to enrol and supervise apprentices and to punish offenders against rules and by-laws decided by the master, wardens and assistants. The way the Company enforced trade rules was through annual 'searches': formal inspection of distillers' premises. Clauses in the charter gave the officials engaged in searches powers of entry and inspection and the right to seize and destroy false measures and 'corrupt and unwholesome' ingredients 'either liquid or spices, seeds, herbs, fruits'. Another clause in the charter gave the Company powers to enter and search starch houses, brew houses and warehouses of anyone preparing 'any wort, wash or dreg' distilled into low wines. An important feature of the power of search was the wide area it was meant to cover. The Distillers' charter gave the Company the power to search within a 21-mile radius of the cities of London and Westminster. This was expanded to 31 miles when a further charter was granted by James II in September 1687.

The establishment of the Distillers' Company took another form. The founders of the Company successfully sought the grant of an elaborate and curious heraldic coat of arms, granted by the Garter King of Arms on

18 March 1639. The arms consist of the sun, with a cloud distilling drops of rain above a double armed still with two worms and receivers with a crest consisting of a barley 'garbe' wreathed by a vine branch bearing grapes. The symbolism of the heraldic supporters, described in the grant as a 'Russe' and an 'Indian savage' is unclear. The two figures may represent the sources of the two main ingredients of the distillers' arts; the 'Russe' representing the importation of Baltic rye and barley, used in distilling of raw spirit and the 'Indian savage' symbolising the sources of the exotic 'botanicals': cardamoms, coriander seed and other herbs and spices used in rectification which were imported from the islands of the 'East Indies'. The Company's motto, specified in the grant of arms, quoted the Book of Deuteronomy: 'Droppe as rain, distill as Dewe'. The grant was a means of publicly establishing the corporate identity of the new organisation.

The Distiller of London

According to the charter of incorporation distilling methods were to be formally regulated according to an official book of rules which was to be drawn up with the approval of Sir Theodore de Mayerne. This was the basis for the publication in 1638 of *The Distiller of London,* a book of recipes and directions for the distillers akin to the official *Pharmacopoeia Londiniensis* used by the Society of Apothecaries. The *Distiller* provides a wealth of insight into the distilling trade. The book lists some twenty different types of distilled strong waters using such ingredients as angelica, marigolds, caraway seeds, lemons, oranges, nutmeg and sweet fennel. Republished by the order of the Company in 1669, 1698 and 1726 *The Distiller of London* laid the basis for the Company's claim to control the trade. The subsequent editions of were published by the Company as a means of buttressing its legal claims, enshrined in the original charter, to regulate distilling in the metropolis.

COAT OF ARMS
granted 18 March 1639

The Apothecaries Resist the Incorporation of the Distillers

Though the Distillers had now obtained a charter from the King, the document had no legal standing in the metropolis unless it had first been formally accepted by the Lord Mayor and Aldermen and enrolled in the City's records. However the new incorporation was seen as a direct threat to the powers of the Society of Apothecaries which vigorously campaigned to overturn the new grant, seeking the support of the Lord Mayor and Aldermen, who showed increasing willingness to resist the creation of a new monopoly by the King.

The Apothecaries launched their denunciation of the new incorporation with a series of allegations against the 'confused multitude of distillers' which they relayed to the Privy Council in September 1638. This complaint alleged that, due to the 'unskillfulness' of the multitude of the distillers, their wares were 'most dangerous for man's health'. The Apothecaries stated that the ranks of the commercial distillers in London consisted of 'sailors, bawds, innkeepers, quack slavers, aliens, men and women, whose honesty and skill are both of no value'. The ingredients used by the distillers were said to be:

> principally the emptying of brewers' vessels, droppings of alewives' taps, washings of beer hogsheads...adding thereunto spices, seeds and herbs, ...dulcifying it with the refuse or dross of sugar, or the dregs of the filthiest remnants of the clarifying of sugar, which is fit only for hog's treacle*

The complaint went on to accuse the Distillers of using artificial colours made of 'turn-sole made of lousy rags gathered in the streets, and taken out of kennels and dunghills...'. These noxious ingredients were used in supposedly inferior lead, brass and copper alembics.

The resulting substances were said to engender 'cancers, virulent agues, plagues, madness'. The Apothecaries' complaint purported that these unhealthy distilled waters had caused numerous deaths aboard the

---

* Feed for pigs which consisted of the residue from sugar refining.

ships of the East India fleet. The strength of these spirits was said to be so great that 'one pint of these waters is so fierce and heady that it will make half a score of men and women drunk'. The Apothecaries complained that 'they baptize their waters, with false and fantasticall strange names, only to allure the ignorant people to drink of those venimous waters'. The complaint listed 31 different 'new minted barbarous names' including such oddities as 'aqua paradisa', 'aqua mirabilis' and 'aqua paracelcsi'. The list demonstrates how commercial distillers used these early examples of brand names to attract custom with the reputed magical and medicinal powers of different disillations.

De Mayerne, Cademan and Brouncker quickly responded to the Apothecaries' assault on the new incorporation by launching a high-toned if not haughty counter-petition which accused the Apothecaries of overstepping the bounds of their own calling and of breaking social decorum by daring to criticise the action of their superiors: '...the Apothecaries having been transgressors, rebelliously exalting the head above the foot'. The counter-petition vigorously denied the Apothecaries' claims and accused them of meddling in a trade in which they were largely ignorant.

The City of London supported the Apothecaries' campaign and, despite repeated and increasingly menacing threats from King Charles, consistently refused to enrol the charter. The City's stance, outlined in a petition to the King in February 1639, was that the new incorporation would infringe the rights of existing livery companies and trades, such as the Vintners, Barber Surgeons and Apothecaries, who also claimed the liberty to distil 'hot waters' and vinegar. Charles I adamantly refused to accept the Corporation's excuses, threatening to use 'some coercive way for despatch of the business, and by that means vindicate his honour'.

The City only relented some twenty years later when in March 1658 the Distillers' charter was at last enrolled. During the intervening years little is known about the status of the Company. The issue of the charter had become bound up with the increasingly deteriorating relationship between the City of London and the Stuart monarchy. The Apothecaries continued their campaign against the new charter by appealing to Parliament in January 1641, at the height of the crisis that was to lead to the Civil War. In the commotion of the next 20 years the powers of the Distillers appear to have been null and void, as the charter languished in the founders' hands. De Mayerne, by now an old man, retired to Chelsea. He died there in 1655 after, it is said, having ingested some tainted wine at a tavern in the Strand. Cademan sought refuge in Royalist Oxford. Brouncker helped Charles to mobilise for war against the Scots. The very existence of the Company during these years may have collapsed in confusion. Freedom records show new members being taken into the Company from September 1638 up to January 1640. Thereafter entries cease, only to be renewed again with new names after 1659. The new entries in the Company's register of members coincide with the City's enrolment of the charter.

'The Company being in its infancy'

The restoration of Charles II in 1660 marked the beginning of a period of renewal in the Company's fortunes. As a first step the Company had its ordinances and by-laws confirmed by the senior law officers of the Crown in 1663. The next fifty years was to see the Company rise to the height of its powers. The Company was evidently starting from a low base. The parlous state of the Company during the early 1660s is attested to by the response of the Court of Assistants to a request by the Lord Mayor in November 1664 for a contribution of £500 towards a £100,000 loan to the King for war against the Dutch. The Company's reply to the request, taking in to account a degree of special pleading, shows how gloomy the prospects of the Company were. The Court

> declared their willingness, but finding themselves to be without lands or tenements or any stock, and consequently can have little credit besides that they are all of other companies, and having but one freeman, and this corporation being in its infancy, cannot possibly comply with the Lord Mayor's Orders.

EIGHT DECANTER LABELS
showing the Company's Coat of Arms

Produced to commemorate the 350th Anniversary
of the Company's Incorporation
1988

The first set was sent to Buckingham Palace as a gift to Her Majesty
Queen Elizabeth II by members of the Livery.

The status of the membership during this period was uncertain. As the reply to the requested contribution suggests, many of the members had retained simultaneous membership of other livery companies. Under the ancient civic principle known as 'the Freedom of London' any member of a livery company was entitled to practise any trade he saw fit, despite the countervailing civic convention which restricted each freeman to the livery company which nominally was in charge of each trade and craft. This tended to blur the distinctions between different trades. Some of the original membership from 1638 appear to have contributed to the reconstitution of the Company. But their numbers were much diminished and had to be supplemented with new members. Enrolment of new members begins in the Company's register of freemen from 1659. The early years of the Restoration appear to have been spent attempting to lure, cajole and coerce practising distillers into the Company's ranks from amongst those who had set up in the trade during the uncertain period of the Interregnum.

Minutes of the meetings of the Court of Assistants, which commence in 1663, show the Distillers' Company trying to assert control of the trade by pursuing and enrolling new members. The records reveal the Court of Assistants issuing summons to all those who had practised the trade in London since the mid-1650s in order to get them to submit to the Company's authority on payment of a fee and to present testimony as to their training and length of time engaged in the trade. An interesting collection of men and women appeared before the Court as a result. They ranged from ex-royalist soldiers to Quakers, elderly widows, Huguenot refugees and Dutch immigrants. Richard Barr, a Quaker of Wapping, told the Court of Assistants in 1663 that he had been a distiller for nine years and that he had 'fell from a clothworker to a distiller by his own ingenuity'. Another Wapping resident, Andrew Smith, stated in the same year that he had 'learnt the trade of an Italian 50 years since'. The Company showed special consideration in the case of a Captain Tombes of Holborn Bridge, who it was recorded had exercised the distillers' trade for five years and was 'very fair in his carriage, the Company are troubled at his incapacity'. In this case the Company waived any entrance fee. Relations with some of the others summoned were not so felicitous. When a Mr. Garroway 'of the Life

Guard near Westminster Abbey' was summonsed in October 1663 he told the Court he had practised distilling for nine years but, according to the Court Minutes, 'he boldly refuseth to give testimony & challengeth their power'. In other instances the Company's request for enrolment was ignored. A man named Darling of Limehouse was said to have 'a great estate' but 'despiseth summons'. If some were reluctant to take up the freedom others actively sought it. Another Quaker, Nicholas Farrell, paid the sum of 55 guineas in 1664 to secure membership. Others gained entry into the freedom of the Company by seeking the assistance of powerful third parties. Three men were admitted to the Company at the behest of Charles II, including his personal distiller, Nicholas Erfurt.

The traditional means by which a livery company gained new members was through the system of apprenticeship. Apprenticeship involved a term of service and training lasting for a minimum of seven years and was the most widely accepted means of teaching skills to urban youth. The apprentices who are recorded in the Distillers' records appear to have come from a very wide variety of social backgrounds ranging from the offspring of yeomen farmers to those of doctors, clergymen and, in one instance, a 'Gentleman of Barbados'. Much of the business of the Court involved the formal enrolment and binding of apprentices to masters, and providing for a new master if the original master died or if, as happened on occasion, relations between masters and apprentices broke down. In such disputes the Company sought to mediate and its intervention could be successful. In one instance a young runaway apprentice was made free of the Company after being formally pardoned by his master. Apprentices were expected both to live and work with their masters. Apprentices were placed in positions of trust, handling cash and stock and, in later years, acting as agents and salesmen. Often apprentices had to give a bond for good behaviour and as the industry expanded in the 18th century the sums involved could be quite substantial. The scale of most distillers' activities remained small with masters keeping on average between one and two apprentices each. Most distilling, even that of the very wealthiest distillers, was carried out at the place of residence. The apprentice was effectively a member of the household of the master.

GRANT OF THE LIVERY
TERCENTENARY APPEAL FUND CUP
1672-1972

107 Liverymen contributed to the Fund

THE BEADLE'S STAVE HEAD

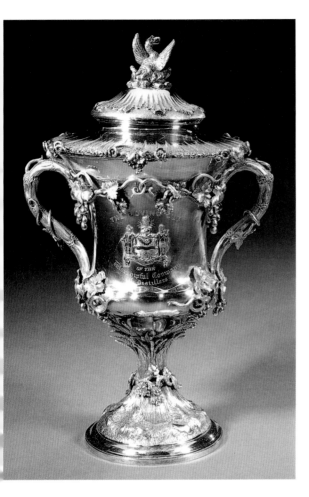

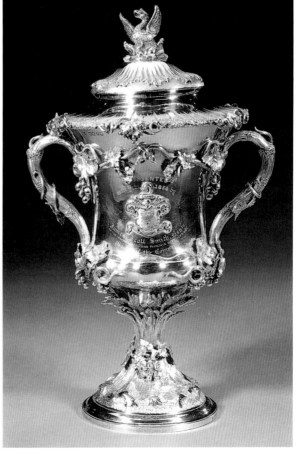

A PAIR OF LOVING CUPS
(showing both sides)

Presented in 1854 by James Scott Smith
of The Whitechapel & Phoenix
Distillery, Master 1849

Note the phoenix on top of the lid

GAVEL
as used by the Master at Court Meetings

Presented by Charles Curtis
Master 1855-1856

Purchased by the Company
to commemorate the
following benefactors to
the Company:

J.A.T. Smyth	1842
J. Vickers	1853
E. Vickers	1857
E. Menzies	1858
J. Nicholson	1861
W. Nicholson	1863
W.F. White	1865
C. Wilson	1866
C. Gordon	1868
G. Orme	1870
T. Browning	1871
J.B. Fleuret	1898
T. P. Dorman	1924

Presented by
James R. Vallentin on 3 April 1900
to commemorate his Mastership 1879-1880
and that of Sir James Vallentin – Sheriff of London and Middlesex –
Master 1869-1870

SOUTH AFRICA MEDAL
with seven clasps

was presented to the Company by H.M. King Edward VII
in commemoration of the part taken by the Company in raising and
equipping the City of London Imperial Volunteers in 1900

FOUR GOBLETS

Master (gold) and Wardens (silver) Goblets

Gift of E. Price Hallowes
Master 1930-1931

PAIR OF QUAICHS

Presented to the Company by
The London Scottish Regiment in 1966

VICTORIAN SILVER GILT ROSE WATER DISH AND EWER
in the form of a baluster still

Presented in 1849 by Joseph Benjamin Claypole, Master

The still is placed on the Master's table at all Company functions.

COMPANY'S SCOTCH WHISKY LABEL
& ENGRAVED TUMBLER

(Note: Bottle size: 75cl. Bottled prior to January 1994
when bottle size was reduced to 70cl by E.E.C. legislation.)

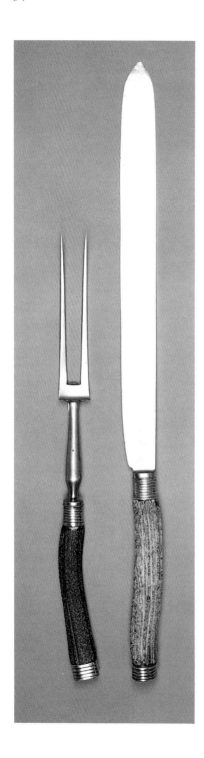

SET OF CARVERS
for Baron of Beef or Ox Roast

Knife nearly 3 feet long
Fork nearly 2 feet long

DIRK
presented by the Chairman and Directors
of the Distillers Company Ltd. (now United Distillers plc)
to mark the Mastership of their colleague
Michael Boileau Henderson
Master 1982-1983

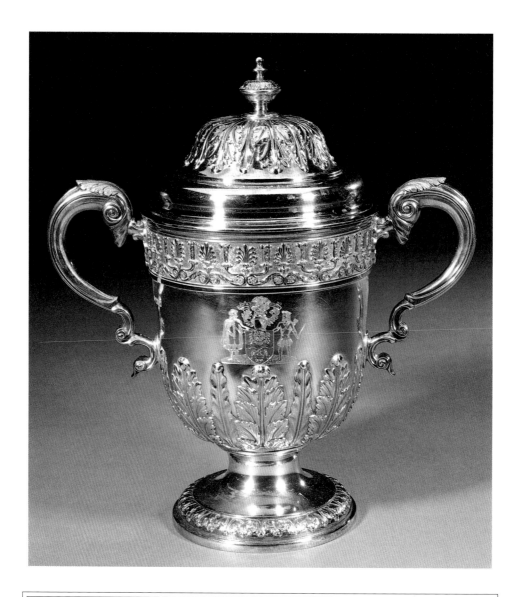

Presented by
The Chairman and Directors of the Distillers Company Ltd.
(now United Distillers plc)
to mark the Mastership of their colleague
Randolph Wemyss Dunsire
Master 1970-1971

The Worshipful Company of Distillers

1638 - 1988

THE MANSION HOUSE
Monday 19th September 1988

MENU FOR THE LADIES BANQUET
held at the Mansion House on 19 September 1988 to celebrate
the 350th Anniversary of the Company's Incorporation

Master: Alan Burrough, C.B.E.
The Lord Mayor: Sir Christopher Collett, C.B.E.

Women as Distillers

An important feature of the distilling trade in the late 17th century was the prominence of women. There are many instances in the Court Minutes of the 1660s and 1670s of women being given licence to practise the art, though they were denied the full rights of membership accorded to freemen. Either as wives, widows or as *femmes soles* women can be found running distilling businesses, taking apprentices and contributing to the Company financially in the Court Minutes. The prominence of women is explained by the nature of the distilling trade. Prior to the introduction of a commercial distilling industry much of the distilling of non-alcoholic 'simple waters' had long been a traditional women's skill which they continued to exercise well after the establishment of a commercial distilling industry. The numbers of women who were licensed by the Company to practise distilling declines in the 18th century. Their disappearance from the records may reflect their exclusion from the industry as a whole.

The case of Judith Robins illustrates the rôle of women in the distilling industry and of their relationship to the Company. She was officially summonsed to appear before the Court of Assistants in November 1666 and when asked by what right she claimed to practise the trade she was reported to have told the Court 'she has used the art 24 years and 3 years as a widow'. She requested admittance as a 'member of this society' and was admitted when she agreed to contribute to the Company's charges in defending abuses by the Farmers of Excise, officials charged with the collection of taxes on commodities such as spirits.

The Company tried either to grant licences to women to practise the trade or to prosecute those who remained unlicensed. Elizabeth Pundlebury, a widow of Ivy Lane, was threatened with prosecution by the Company in October 1681 when it was found she had compounded to pay the Farmers of the Excise without the Company's knowledge. When confronted by the Court she admitted to distilling 'simple waters and syrups' as well as four gallons of strong waters. The widows of distillers often continued to practise the trade in their own right, sometimes after remarriage, and the Company frequently sanctioned this. When an upholsterer John Jeames, who had married a Widow Burly, was brought before the Court in August 1666 and asked by what right he exercised the trade, he alleged 'he used it not but his wife used it for the good of her and her children'. Marriage to the widow of a Distiller was a means of gaining entry into the Company. Other men testified before the Company that they had learnt the trade from women and there are several instances in the Court minutes of boys being apprenticed to women. The rôle of women in this period and their subsequent disappearance from the trade as the 18th century progressed is striking and worthy of further research.

A growing membership expanded the business and ceremonial life of the Company. Day-to-day Company administration centred on the activities of the Clerk who was both a member and an employee of the Company. The Clerk was an important figure who often was the Company's chief representative in negotiation with official bodies. He was assisted by the Beadle or ceremonial serjeant-at-arms who officiated at all important events. The Beadle in turn was assisted by an under Beadle, who in 1683 was the young son of a member. For Company feasts and dinners, stewards and ushers were appointed from among junior liverymen. These posts involved time and expense for stewards and ushers were expected both to oversee arrangements for dinners and to contribute towards their costs. Inevitably this led to refusals to serve and fines were exacted against offenders. On occasion the Court could act with seeming harshness. When in July 1695 the wife of an absent steward, one Francis Jackman, sent a letter stating that her husband was at Bath 'for his health' the Court voted not to allow this excuse and ordered the man to return to his post. The Court of Assistants also took periodic measures to discipline its own ranks. This self-policing could be quite strict. Fines were exacted for such offences against decorum as failing to wear the livery gown on election day meetings, absence and late arrival at meetings. The money thus collected was placed in the Company's Poor Box. Persistent absence led to dismissal from the Court. In May 1682 the unfortunate Brian Bordler was discharged as Warden when it was reported he had 'gone beyond the seas' to avoid his creditors.

As membership of the Company built up in the 1660s and 1670s the Court of Assistants turned to other pressing matters. The central purpose of the Company was the regulation of the trade and to this end the Company used a variety of means, carrying out public inspections, supporting members involved in law suits, hiring informers to seek out illicit distilling or 'interlopers', and lobbying the City Corporation, the Crown and Parliament to strengthen the Company's interests. Two important achievements enhanced the Company's authority. The grant of a livery in November 1671 by the City Corporation and the new charter granted by James II on 13 September 1687 were two significant developments which increased both the Company's powers and its public rôle. The grant of a livery entitled the Company to take a full part in civic elections, and the elaborate public ceremonies that attended them, and gave the membership the right to wear the livery gown and hood, an ancient symbol of corporate affiliation on all such occasions. Thenceforth the Distillers took its place alongside the other livery companies at the great civic pageants which attended the election of the Lord Mayor of London.

The new charter of 1687 went further by extending the powers of public inspection to 31 miles of the City. The right to exercise public inspections or searches of distillers' premises was one of the most powerful tools in the hands of the Company. Four times yearly the Company officers, accompanied by the beadle bearing the Company's silver-topped staff, would assemble in different parts of the City and with an element of high ceremony perambulate the streets going from still room to dram shop, testing measures and tasting samples from each. Fines were issued for offences such as short measures and 'foul and weak wares'. The charter of 1687 was confirmed by William and Mary in 1690.

Another interest of the Company during this period was taxation. Almost from its inception the Distillers' Company was the main vehicle by which the commercial distillers of London sought to influence the formation of the policies of King and Parliament with regard to the industry. The fiscal device of the Restoration state of leasing or 'farming' the right to collect the excise—a tax placed on different commodities including

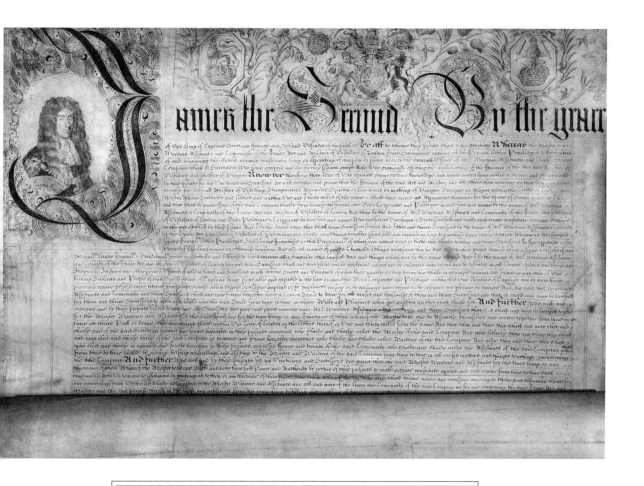

CHARTER

granted to the Company by James II.

12 May 1687

distilled spirits, drew the Distillers' Company into an arduous and prolonged confrontation with the Farmers of the Excise, the men who had paid the Crown for these lucrative rights.

Throughout the 1660s, '70s and '80s the Distillers engaged in protracted negotiations with the Excise Farmers over the rate of duty payable and the application of these duties to different distilled spirits. This lengthy series of disputes involved the Company in a vigorous struggle to maintain its chartered rights, petitioning the House of Commons and the Privy Council, defending Company members against law suits brought by the Farmers, and treating directly with the Farmers themselves to purchase the right to collect duties on drinks such as so called 'low wines', French and 'English' brandy and aqua vitae. The outcome of these activities was to increase the importance of the Company as a representative of the commercial distillery in the eyes of government, and to bind closely the interests of the Company with the progress of legislation which affected the trade.

The Search for a Hall

The acquisition of a hall was to be another essential aim of the Distillers in the years of renewal. The lack of a suitable place to hold meetings posed a dilemma for the Court of the Distillers' Company in this period of its 'infancy'. The ability to raise a fund for the building of a hall was based on the collective wealth of the membership. But it proved difficult to persuade and cajole commercial distillers to join the organisation when the 'Freedom of London' permitted any man free of another livery company to practise any trade that he wished. The lack of a hall as a centre for the administration of the Distillers' affairs and for ceremonial dinners would have been a disincentive to take up the freedom of the Company.

During these years the Company's meetings were peripatetic, assembling in the rented halls of other established livery companies, including the

Stationers, Saddlers, Painter Stainers and Cooks, as well as inns, taverns and the newly popular coffee houses. On occasions the Company would hold meetings at the house of the current Master, as in April 1664 when the Court assembled at the house of the current Master Joseph Wells by 'his order'. It would appear from the Company's court minutes that the Distillers met for a time at the house of the Clerk, John Greene, who in April 1665 was directed by the Court of Assistants to take up the lease of an alehouse adjoining his premises for Company meetings. Though no meetings of the Company were held for six months from June 1665 to January 1666 due to the onset of the Great Plague, the court minutes record that, for a short time after, the Company appeared to have the semblance of a meeting place.

The use of the Clerk's house and the adjoining alehouse was to lead later generations of Distillers to believe in a 'lost' hall which was destroyed in the Great Fire of London. The Company's minutes for 9 March 1666 contain the heading 'New Hall'. But the new adjoining building appears to have been inadequate as in August of the same year the Court Minutes record that the Company were meeting at the Cooks' Hall. Further confusion is added to the question as to whether the Company had a hall at this date by the language used in the official grant of the right to wear livery, promulgated by the City Corporation in 1671, which stated that the Company should be enjoined to build a hall 'which was burnt or demolished in the late dismal fire'. Whatever the reason for abandoning the Clerk's house, the oven fire which famously began in Pudding Lane on 3 September 1666 and which was to destroy two-thirds of the area within the walls of the City of London was to force the Distillers to search for a haven yet again.

In the rubble of the ruined city the Company took the decision to join collectively to raise money for the purchase of property for a hall. On 6 September 1669 a William Simmons agreed to make a gift of 10,000 bricks towards the building of a hall and on the same day some forty members of the Company subscribed to an agreement which bound them to pay sums ranging between £7 and £20 each for the building of a hall 'which will be for the honour of the said city, and the splendour, good estate and welfare of the said Company'. On 20 September the Court of Assistants took the decision *'nemine contradicente'*, forthwith to build a hall and appointed a committee to oversee the project. The sums were agreed to be paid in three instalments; one when the purchase of a suitable piece of ground was agreed, one at the laying down of the first foundation and a final payment on completion. The total amount raised by this means is difficult to verify. The absence of the Company's minutes between 1670 and 1675 makes it impossible to say what, if anything, was done with this fund. The Company accounts for these years reveal that a 'Free Gift and Subscription' fund was slowly built up.

In May 1680 another committee was appointed to negotiate with individuals to purchase a site, and in March 1681 it agreed to buy a site in Thames Street from a Mr. Millson for £165. This sum corresponds to the amount placed in the Company's 'Free Gift and Subscription' in the intervening years. The Thames Street site was almost immediately let out to a Mr. Watson at £9 per annum by the Company on a 61-year building lease, which meant that the decision to build a hall was postponed. In the meantime the Company was to benefit substantially from leasing out the Thames Street property as a sugar baker's house. The search for a hall was to be an abiding concern of later generations of Distillers.

Despite the lack of a hall, the Distillers' Company emerged from this period with its *raison d'être* fully established. The size of the livery grew from 52 in 1683 to over 100 in 1699. The profits from fines on 'interlopers', contributions both voluntarily and involuntarily exacted on members, and the income from the Thames Street property all meant that corporate finances were secured, and a stock of cash built up. There is an air of self confidence in the Company's affairs in the 1680s and 1690s, reflected in the Company's participation in the elaborate public ceremonies which marked the yearly election of the Lord Mayor. The Renter Wardens' Accounts for these years show yearly payments for coloured ribbons, gloves, and music, as well as, on occasion, wine and oysters for the livery. Corporate self-esteem of this period was reflected in the purchase of a silken standard bearing the Company's coat of arms and the provision of a silver head for the Company's staff. In the succeeding generation members of the Distillers' Company were to be counted amongst the most wealthy and powerful manufacturing interests in England. The status of the Company reflected the social prestige and wealth of its members. Though the Distillers counted many a back-street trader 'stilling' a few gallons a month for a humble living, the Company was dominated by the wealthiest practitioners. Samuel Johnson, observing the industry at the height of the trade in the mid-18th century, thought 'the great fortunes recently made were to him convincing proof that the trade of distilling was the most profitable of any now exercised in the kingdom except that of being the Prime Minister'. The growing status of the Company, and the wealth and social profile of individual members, was reflected by the assumption by liverymen of civic office. Two members of the Distillers became Aldermen; John Green served between 1718 and 1721 and Robert Blunt served between 1761 and 1763. If the Company had earlier been something of a *parvenu* amongst the older, more established livery companies, then by the beginning of the 18th century it had taken its place alongside the more ancient guilds in civic life.

The Growth of the Trade: The Distillers' Company during 'the Gin Age'

Between the Glorious Revolution and the reign of the Hanoverians a colossal expansion in demand for the products of the London distillers occurred as various sections of English society developed a taste for the new 'strong waters'. The replacement of the House of Stuart by William of Orange brought to the Throne one who enjoyed the juniper-flavoured spirit of his native Netherlands. *Genever* was anglicised to 'Geneva' and, later shortened to gin, became popular among William's entourage. The aristocratic taste for cordials, punches, brandy and, above all, gin began to be shared by other levels of society. 'Geneva' replaced beer and ale as the favourite drink of the poor as dram-shops and gin-shops proliferated in London and its suburbs. Contemporaries noted a marked change in English drinking habits. Charles Davenant commented in the early 1690s: ' 'Tis a growing vice among the common people, and may in time prevail as much as opium with the Turks'. Throughout this period of expansion the Distillers' Company strove, with diminishing success, to maintain control of the trade as granted in the charter of James II.

As the distilling industry expanded so too did the built-up area of the metropolis which lay outside their control. The industry developed into two distinct branches: malt distillers who produced large quantities of raw spirit, and compound distillers who purchased the product of the malt distillers and then 'rectified' the raw spirit into various spirituous liquors which they then sold on. The Distillers' Company came to represent the wealthier malt distillers and rectifiers who either sold on raw spirits to smaller more numerous compound distillers, or sold their products through licensed premises.

By the 1730s London was said to have 1,500 distillers, of whom a hundred had equipment worth more than £1,000, in addition to something like 1,200 smaller distillers using stills worth less than £100. The expansion in the consumption of spirituous liquors altered the fortunes of the Distillers' Company in a way that the original founders would have scarcely believed credible. What had begun as an adjunct to the apothecaries' trade, dealing mainly in distillations for medicinal purposes, was transformed into one of London's most important industries.

Domestic production rose from half a million gallons in the mid-1680s to over eight million gallons in the 1740s. Several factors accounted for the growth of the industry during this period. Most important was the attitude of the new Williamite administration and the successive governments that followed in the early 18th century during the period of the ascendancy of the Whigs in Parliament. The ban imposed on the importation of spirits following declaration of war against France by William of Orange in 1689 prompted a take-off in domestic production as well as an increase in the 'running' or smuggling of French brandy. Parliament created a

Trade card of an 18th-
century London Distiller
(Museum of London).

series of new Acts which were specifically intended to promote the distilling
industry. Legislation in 1690 permitted anyone to set up a distillery after
giving 10 days' notice to the Excise. This opening up of the trade to those
not free of the City of London and the Distillers' Company exposed the
membership of the Company to competition, though during the initial
period of growth both free and 'interloper' distillers prospered.

Further legislation in Queen Anne's reign exempted the 'interlopers'
from the requirement that they serve seven-year apprenticeships before
setting up in the trade. The low level of excise duty paid on spirituous
liquor gave a further advantage to the distillers. Until 1729 the rate was
1d. per gallon, as compared with duties on 'strong beer', which rose from
2d. per quart in the late 1680s to more than 3d. in the 1720s. The retailing
end of the trade was also opened up as retail distillers were exempted

from the licensing system imposed on alehouses. Cheaper grain prices due to better harvests from the 1690s onwards gave an added boost to the industry by keeping down production costs. Distilling came to be seen by successive governments as a buttress to England's agricultural landowners and farmers who found a ready market for their surpluses. In 1713 Daniel Defoe hailed the distilling of corn in time of plenty as 'one of the most essential things to support the landed interest that any branch of trade can help us to, and therefore especially to be preserved and tenderly used'. Parliament initially tended to agree with this sentiment.

As the period of expansion progressed, the Company fought an increasingly losing battle to preserve its control of the industry. A prime means of exercising control was through the enforcement of the right of search: the periodic public inspections of the area covered by the 21-mile jurisdiction granted in the Company's original charter. Throughout the 1690s and 1700s the Company officers would perambulate the City streets, enforcing fines for sub-standard products and going to law against those who resisted these rights of inspection. In 1698 Walsingham Heathfield was sued in the Court of Common Pleas after refusing to pay a fine of £3 imposed on him 'for abusing the Master and Warden Henning upon a search and giving them very bad language telling them they made a rogue and villain free & had acted unjustly'. He later meekly appeared before the Court and declared himself 'very sorry for his offence'. An example of the fines received from various searches carried out between early May and mid-June 1715 gives an indication of the sums involved, and incidentally reveals the most important location for trading distillers in the metropolitan area:

	£	s	d
South West	3	2	0
West	7	11	4
East	2	8	4
South East	3	8	4
East Smithfield	4	12	0
London	5	8	8
West Smithfield	6	5	0

The growth of the metropolis and the proliferation of back-street dram and gin shops posed considerable problems of enforcement. The Company's right to search was increasingly subject to suits by individuals challenging the search as a restraint of trade. Though searches were continued in the first decades of the 18th century, the practice appears increasingly subject to question. In February 1723 the Court of the Company debated 'whether the searches be continued for the future'. Though the issue was not immediately resolved, the records of the Court of Assistants after this date carry no trace of any further enforcement.

Another means by which the Company sought to maintain its chartered rights was subjecting 'interlopers' to Company by-laws. This was done through the issuing of summonses to individuals to attend the Court of Assistants in order to demonstrate their right to trade openly. In April 1694 the Court heard that one Charles Loving 'confesses he does distill fruit and molasses but hath noe right'. As with the search the legal position of the Company was increasingly uncertain. In 1704 the Court appointed a committee to 'advise with Councel touching prosecuting interlopers'. As well as taking interlopers to law the Company also was prepared to take on the costs of defending individual members who found themselves subject to court action, and was ready to go further. In June 1715 the Court of Assistants ordered the Company to pay for the costs of prosecuting anyone who 'shall be concerned in the molesting or troubling any free distiller'. Yet the Company's claim to control the trade was increasingly being undermined by the explosion in numbers of interloping distillers as laws designed to stimulate the industry undermined Company control. Nevertheless the Company continued to act as vehicle for a significant section of the malt distillers and the larger firms of rectifiers.

The Company actively pursued the interests of the commercial distillers by influencing Parliamentary legislation on the industry. From the 1690s the Court of Assistants directed that the Master, Wardens and named individual members regularly meet to oversee the Company's lobbying efforts. As the volume of legislation affecting the industry increased, the ad-hoc committee was given more powers. Parliamentary action against smugglers was promoted in 1717 when the Court ordered that the Masters and Wardens be empowered 'to borrow such sums of money as they shall think fit to raise for carrying on the bill against the running of brandy'. From this period the Company regularly appointed a solicitor to watch out for impending legislation and to help draw up briefs for the advice of counsel as to how to influence the formation of new Acts. The Company's attempts to influence Parliament became even more important as the legislative climate changed in the second and third decades of the 18th century.

The privileges accorded to the distilling trade by legislation began to be challenged in the early 18th century. Increasing disquiet was being voiced by local magistrates about the effects of spirit drinking. A vigorous public campaign, aligned to movements for religious and moral reform promoted by such groups as the Society for Propagation of Christian Knowledge (founded 1704), attacked the popular consumption of spirituous liquors as a source of public drunkenness, profanity and sin. Gin drinking by the poor was singled out as the scourge of the metropolis; the source of high mortality rates, abandoned children, riots and disorders by 'the mob'. As the Westminster Justices reported to the Government in 1721, the consumption of gin and other spirituous liquors was 'the principal cause of the increase of our poor and of all the vice and debauchery among the inferior sort of people, as well as of the felonies and other disorders committed in and about this town'. The prevalence of gin drinking by the poor was also blamed for causing the death of children and infants through neglect by parents leading to malnutrition. It is difficult to assess the reality of such claims. Other factors such as housing conditions, bad sanitation and diseases such as smallpox and typhoid fever may have been greater sources of high levels of infant mortality in the metropolis; but what is clear is that alcohol consumption became the focus of anxiety about social problems whose root causes could be said to lie elsewhere.

The chorus of concern rose to a crescendo in the 1730s when a vigorous campaign against gin consumption succeeded in pushing through Parliament a series of Acts designed to regulate and limit the retailing of spirits, beginning with the famous Gin Act of 1736. This legislation placed a duty of 20s. a gallon on gin and other spirits and required retailers to take out a licence of £50. The new Act also set up a system of paid informers, a system which proved so unpopular that it had to be abandoned.

The Distillers' Company was put in a difficult position by the public campaign against gin drinking, and the subsequent legislative measures adopted by Parliament. On the one hand it attempted to defend the interests of its members, mounting intense lobbying of Parliament and the Corporation of London to modify the new Acts and providing legal assistance to members who were prosecuted under the legislation. At the same time the Company was concerned not to be seen to be fostering the worst aspects of gin consumption, especially the retailing of drink in small dram shops and by itinerant street traders. In the run-up to legislation in 1729, which proposed a licence fee of £20 for retailers and a duty of 2s. a gallon on spirits, the Court of Assistants decided to

> prepare a Representation to be made public, & inserted in some paper to signify the Company's good inclination to prevent the excessive drinking of any distilled liquors to the damage of the common people and likewise do declare the fallacy that is commonly received of making use of ingredients in the said liquors to the prejudice of the healths of the people.

The 1729 Act was repealed three years later. The reformers then mounted a new campaign for stricter legislation. A vociferous stream of pamphlets issued forth with such titles as *Spirituous Liquors, the Bane of the Nation.* The Company responded with a public campaign of its own, paying for the publishing, printing and distribution of a reply to *Spirituous Liquors.* At the same time it employed several Parliamentary agents to lobby M.P.s and peers in an attempt to modify aspects of any new Bill. Despite these efforts, a new Bill raising the costs of duties and licences passed through the House of Commons and the House of Lords.

Before the Gin Act became law in September the streets and alleys of the metropolis witnessed strange scenes of mock funeral processions of

A funeral procession for 'Madame Geneva' with distillers in attendance.
(Museum of London)

gin drinkers mourning the 'death' of 'Mother Geneva'. Dram shops and gin shops were draped with black crêpe in her honour. The administration of Robert Walpole suspected Jacobites of fomenting the protests, by writing anonymous letters to distillers, encouraging them to distribute free gin to the London crowds to mark the new Act, but this was never proven. The new Act failed to fulfil its intended purposes, merely driving the poorer distillers underground, and was eventually superseded by new Acts of Parliament. It was only with renewed campaigning in the late 1740s and early 1750s that workable legislation was finally enacted.

The enactment of the new legislation marked a turning point in the Company's history. The Company increasingly turned its attention away from protecting the interests of the distilling trade as a whole and participating in national debates such as marked the 1730s and 1740s. With income from the Thames Street sugar house and the accumulation of several thousand pounds worth of stock, the Company turned in on itself, concentrating on the administration of its corporate resources, doling out small pensions to individual members, and celebrating its new-found corporate wealth in convivial dinners and meals. The bill of fare for 42 persons at a dinner held on the day of election of the Lord Mayor for 1754, recorded in the Clerk's memoranda book, gives a sense of the lavish cuisine of the time as well as the wealth of the Company:

2 roasted & boned fowls and oysters and a large ham
1 Turkey & 2 chines
3 dishes of minced pies
2 tongues & 2 udders
2 dishes marrow puddings
2 geese, a chump of beef
2 pigeon with chump rib steaks
3 dishes of wild fowl
3 apple pies
5 stands of fruit

As the Company enjoyed this bounty, its close association with the trade underwent a radical transformation. Slowly but surely the economic and social forces which were profoundly changing English society were undermining the older system of economic regulation by guild and livery company. By degrees the Company's connection with the trade profoundly changed. The interest in protecting the trade seems to have waned. Innovative proposals which would have benefited the trade, such as the idea of setting up a fire insurance scheme for members presented to the Court of Assistants in 1734, were rejected, in this case because this proposal exceeded the terms of the charter of incorporation. The last attempt at influencing legislation came in 1757 when the Company contemplated a proposal to apply to Parliament for some mitigation against the total prohibition of corn distilling, undertaken the previous year due to the high price of corn. Though the Company later discussed the resolutions passed by the House of Commons regarding the lifting of the stoppage of corn distilling in 1760, thereafter the Company made no further efforts at lobbying Parliament on behalf of the industry.

The changing nature of the distilling industry worked against the diversified character of the trade, and the older associations between the industry and the Company. In the wake of the public outcry over gin drinking, successive limitations were placed on the distilling industry by Parliament, forbidding distillers from retailing their products and imposing higher duties levied prior to returns from sales. The cumulative effects of the new legislation worked against the smaller rectifiers who were slowly and remorselessly driven to the wall. This legislative climate worked to the advantage of the larger firms who were better able to pay the new duty and had connections to retail outlets. The distillers who triumphed in this period were large-scale entrepreneurs who founded new firms which gave rise to the great distilling houses of the Victorian period. Distilling ceased to be carried out in the household of the distiller as large purpose-built distilleries were built, often situated on the very fringes of the metropolitian area in suburban Kent, Surrey and Middlesex. Many of the men who created these firms were not members of the Company. The formation of an informal 'Rectifiers' Club', which met regularly at the *City of London Tavern* from the late 1780s to discuss matters relating to the trade, signalled the loosening connections between the Company and the trade. Interestingly the same *City of London Tavern* was also used extensively for Company meetings and dinners during this period. It was not till the early 19th century, when the winds of political reform blew through all of London's civic institutions, that the Distillers once again took an active part in the affairs of London.

The loosening of the connection with the trade can be seen in the declining numbers of freemen in the late 18th century. In September 1773 the Court of Assistants took into consideration 'the great decrease of members of the Company', and a month later complained to the Court

Interior of the *City of London Tavern*, site of meetings of the Distillers in the 19th century. George Augustus Sala, *Twice Around the Clock*, 1858. (Museum of London)

of Common Council that because of the transfer of members of the distilling trade to other livery companies the Distillers 'are greatly diminished in number', and that the Company had been forced to abandon the office of steward. Fear was expressed that in a few years it would be difficult to make up the numbers necessary to hold Courts of Assistants.

New Members for Old

The Court of Common Council responded with a new civic bye-law, passed in September 1774, which required all practising distillers of spirits and vinegar in the City to take up the freedom of the Company. Though the Company used this Act of Common Council to try to force those outside the Company to join, the problem continued. The later decades of the 18th century were marked by inquorate meetings, summonses to non-freemen to join, and postponed elections. In October 1789 the Court of Assistants noted the 'great inconvenience which has frequently occurred to the Company's affairs for want of such a number of Assistants as are required by their charter'. One member of the Court, who it was alleged to have failed to turn up to meetings for 10 years, was asked to resign from the court. The Company responded with both the carrot and the stick. A system of fees payable to Assistants was instituted to induce better attendance. But the problem of poor attendance continued. Attempts were made to force the business partners of freemen to join the Company under the Act of 1774 and this succeeded in inducing several men to join.

The Company went further in pursuit of new members. The Court commenced prosecution against Samuel Bishop in April 1783 for setting up in the business of a distiller in Bread Street after he refused to heed a summons, reportedly saying 'he did not choose to take up his freedom, nor did he think himself liable thereto'. Bishop later relented and joined the Company. In the 1780s the Company used the method of summons and threatened prosecution to force a number of commercial distillers to join its ranks, and to pay the redemptioners' set fee of £6. This succeeded in bringing into the freedom a new generation of members who were later to dominate the Company's affairs. These men were members of the more successful of the malt and rectifying firms. In the late 1780s and early 1790s a number of prominent distillers took up the freedom, including John Bockett, one of the largest of the metropolitan malt and rectifying distillers, Alexander Gordon, founder of the illustrious firm of that name, Samuel Liptrap, the first member to take on the office of Sheriff in 1795,

Interior of an 18th-century distillery from Malachy Postlethwaite's
Supplement to the Universal Dictionary, 1754. (Museum of London)

and George Scholey, who went on in 1812 to be the first member of the
Distillers' Company to become Lord Mayor of London. Scholey's mayoralty
was a quiet one for the Company, the conditions of war placing a limit
on civic celebration. His time in office is best remembered in a series of
satirical cartoons directed against him for his interventions in the issue
of Catholic emancipation and the high price of corn. Nevertheless Scholey's
elevation to high office signalled the beginning of a renewed involvement
by members of the Company in the affairs of the City.

This new intake of freemen signalled a more general attempt to
renew connections with the trade and to revive the Company's fortunes.
In the aftermath of the Napoleonic wars the Company set about issuing
summonses under the 1774 Act to practising distillers and vinegar makers
in the metropolitan area to join the Company. In July 1826 the Company
called upon some 78 to take up the freedom by redemption. Though 53
initially failed to respond, some 31 men took up the offer, paying a flat
fee of £6. Among these new members were still more of the metropolis's
larger commercial distillers, men such as James Lys Seagar and William

Evans, founders of the firm of Seagar, Evans, & Co., distillers at Millbank, whose prominence in the Company's affairs mirrored their importance as commercial distillers. In the 1830s and 1840s members of the most famous distilling houses joined the Company's ranks, including Edward Tanqueray, distiller of Vine Street, Bloomsbury free by redemption in 1835, and Sir Felix Booth free by redemption in 1849. This attempt at renewing links with the trade, coinciding with calls for political reform of the electoral system of the City of London, did much to revive the importance of the Company. Yet this attempt at renewal involved a sometimes painful adjustment to changing circumstances.

This era was one of war, followed by political agitation which led to the reform of the 'ancient' institutions, such as the livery companies, which honeycombed the operation of local and central government. These organisations were subjected to close Parliamentary scrutiny and new legislation. Calls for constitutional reform of British parliamentary institutions, culminating in the Great Reform Act of 1832, were mirrored at the local level by attacks by municipal reform movements on the political powers of the Corporation of London and the livery companies. The first challenge to the livery companies came in the form of an investigation into their affairs by the Royal Commission on Municipal Corporations, appointed in July 1833. The Distillers' Company, unlike some of the other London livery companies, responded with alacrity to the Commissioners' request for information, producing detailed if sometimes less than revealing answers to their queries. The Master reported to the Court that he was 'fully satisfied' with the Company's reply to the Commission. The livery companies and the City Corporation escaped the proposed reforms when new legislation was passed for other towns and cities in England and Wales in 1837 but the impetus for reform continued as municipal reformers from the 1850s onwards pressed for changes in the political powers and corporate wealth of the livery companies.

Amidst the political agitation of the 1830s the Company moved to the forefront of civic life. In September 1837 the Company took an active part in celebrations to mark the crowning of Queen Victoria. A stand in

St Paul's Churchyard was constructed, draped with cloth in the Company's colours. An elaborate procession by the Company was mounted through the main streets of the City, lovingly detailed in the Court Minutes, which consisted of the entire Company, richly arrayed in livery gowns, escorted by costumed standard bearers and the Yeomen of the Guard, all accompanied to the strains of a detachment of the band of the Grenadier Guards. It was a triumph of antiquarian inspired pageantry and it cost £200, a sum that was to be complained of in the years to come, when corporate finances were low. In 1855 it was decided that no attendance fees be paid to Court members till the sum was compensated to the Company's account. But on the occasion the Company was pleased. Dinner was afterwards provided in the *City of London Tavern* and, as the description in the Court minutes ends, 'the evening was passed with great conviviality, and a long and happy reign to Her Most Gracious Majesty was toasted with utmost enthusiasm'.

Inauguration of Lord Mayor Johnson, 1845 (*Illustrated London News*).

The high point of the Company's prominence in the public life of the City came when two freemen of the Company were chosen as Sheriff and Lord Mayor. Unlike the earlier limited celebrations for Samuel Liptrap and George Scholey, the Company appears to have decided on grand public demonstrations. Grandiose celebrations were staged to mark the installation of William Evans as Sheriff of London in 1839 and John Johnson as Lord Mayor in 1845. The Company evinced its civic pride by elaborate preparations and expenditure and on the appointed days in grandiose public displays. On both occasions the Company celebrated with a procession through the streets of London, taking a ceremonial barge journey from the City to Westminster Hall, where the Sheriffs and the Lord Mayor were presented to the Crown's representatives.

This corporate esteem for its members who held high office was to be put to the test. William Evans and his fellow Sheriff Wheelton were to take a dramatic if minor rôle in the long struggle to establish the legal right to print the proceedings of the House of Commons. In November 1839 both men were imprisoned by the Serjeant-at-Arms of the House of Commons after the Sheriffs attempted to arrest the official printer to the House of Commons, John Hansard, who had been found guilty of libel in publishing animadversions on fellow printer, John Stockdale, in an official parliamentary report. The Sheriffs' intervention was considered in contempt of the jurisdiction of the House of Commons. The Company responded remarkably to Evans's predicament, offering a fulsome expression of 'their unfeigned admiration of the firm, upright and honourable manner in which he and his colleague Mr. Sheriff Wheelton have deported themselves in their exertions'. This expression of solidarity was delivered in person to the two Sheriffs incarcerated in the prison rooms of the House of Commons by a delegation of the Company, dressed for the occasion, in their livery gowns. Evans and Wheelton both thanked them for their visit 'so gratifying a mark of their esteem and sympathy'. Evans and Wheelton were released to the general acclaim of the City. An Act of Parliament passed the next year gave protection against libel action to persons publishing papers printed by order of Parliament.

The support shown for Evans came at the height of renewal of the Company's association with the trade and involvement in the life of the City in the 19th century. The closeness of the renewal can be seen in the decision of William Evans's partner, the equally eminent commercial distiller James Lys Seagar, to bind his son as apprentice to his partner and fellow liveryman. New apprenticeships under the Company's auspices had been dwindling for some time. Nevertheless even for these large-scale entrepreneurs, apprenticeship was still considered relevant to the training of young men in the distilling trade. In the years to come apprenticeship was to decline even more dramatically, and after 1858 no apprentices were enrolled in the Company until the early 1960s, when the practice was revived.*

The Second Search for a Hall

Amidst these efforts at renewal in the Company's connections with the trade, and public clamour for reform, another attempt was made to found a hall. In July 1835 an enthusiastic younger member of the Court of Assistants, James Scott Smith, submitted a proposal for building a hall costing between £10,000 and £15,000, including rough elevations provided by an architect friend. Smith's intention, set out in a letter to the Court, was that the Distillers' Company might, by possessing a hall, 'enjoy that "otium cum dignitate" to which they are in every sense of the word so much entitled'. In October of the same year the Company responded by setting up a committee to look into previous attempts at founding a hall and possible steps towards renewing such efforts.

The committee's report, submitted in October 1835, provides an insight into the position of a livery company in an era of the triumph of an economic system which had eradicated the reasons for its existence. The Distillers' Company could no longer in any meaningful sense be said to represent the commercial industry as a whole in deliberations with official bodies set up to regulate the trade. But membership in the Company was still seen to be related to the industry in a very particular way. The

---

* Since that time several liverymen have chosen to enrol their sons as apprentices.

committee contemplated the Company's formal rôle in regulating the trade but counselled caution in any attempt to revive old powers

> by endeavouring to re-animate some of its dormant powers, or by calling again into existence and operation many of its earliest usages; lapse of time and change of circumstances have materially rendered many of its customs obsolete, and the exercise of some portions of its jurisdiction incompatible with the present system of trade.

Nevertheless the committee reported that membership in the Company was still relevant to many in the trade and that, as in the past, the Company had 'enrolled amongst its members many of the most respectable and influential, as also wealthy individuals engaged in those trades'. The report recommended 'it is expedient that the former attempts be renewed' and proposed a scheme to raise funds.

The scheme proposed that the Company actively set about recruiting new members from the distilling and vinegar making trades, and that the Court solicit support from the most prominent members of the industry both inside and outside the Company. A permanent committee was to be set up in order to collect subscriptions to a separate 'Hall Fund', which, when an adequate amount had been secured, was to be invested in government securities. The Hall scheme was also specifically linked to a renewal of the links with the industry. The scheme proposed that 'it should be an intimation to the trade of distillers and vinegar makers, that the hall, if erected, would be rendered convenient for meetings on matters connected with their trades'. But at the last moment the Court of Assistants had second thoughts and voted to postpone consideration and the proposal was shelved.

Hope for the acquisition of a hall was revived in 1849 when James Scott Smith became Master. Smith proposed to revive the scheme of 1835 and after this was approved by the Court he set about his project with all his earlier enthusiasm. He personally canvassed the livery as to their ideas and reported 'a very general opinion prevailed, that it [the hall] would be well worthy the high character, importance, and great respectability

Report on 'Rebuilding'
the Hall, 1849.

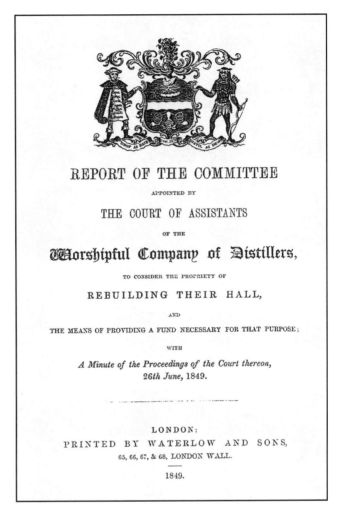

REPORT OF THE COMMITTEE

APPOINTED BY

THE COURT OF ASSISTANTS

OF THE

Worshipful Company of Distillers,

TO CONSIDER THE PROPRIETY OF

REBUILDING THEIR HALL,

AND

THE MEANS OF PROVIDING A FUND NECESSARY FOR THAT PURPOSE;

WITH

A Minute of the Proceedings of the Court thereon,
26th June, 1849.

LONDON:
PRINTED BY WATERLOW AND SONS,
65, 66, 67, & 68, LONDON WALL.

1849.

of the Company, and of the Distillery trade in all its branches'. To this end, Smith, assisted by the Wardens and the 'active and zealous' James Lys Seagar, collected subscriptions from 16 men of sums ranging from £20 to £105. Five men, including Smith himself and Sir Felix Booth, contributed sums of £100 or more each. By this means some £1,100 was built up. The Court of Assistants resolved in June 1849 forthwith to use the sums collected as the nucleus of the proposed 'Hall Fund' which was henceforth to be kept separate and distinct from all other Corporate accounts 'to be sacred to the objects to which it is formed'. The Company proudly and hopefully printed the results of their proceedings and distributed this to the firms of metropolitan corn distillers, with a covering letter inviting them to subscribe to the fund. Another boost to the project achieved by Smith was securing the transfer of the rental income of the Thames Street property, now converted to warehouses and an ironmonger's, to the account of the 'Hall Fund'.

The results of all these exertions must have been a disappointment to all concerned. The original subscription was invested in government stocks and over the next 10 years the modest sum of £2,325 was gathered in the fund. The indomitable James Scott Smith died in June 1864 and, with what appears to be somewhat indecent haste, the Court decided to transfer back the rental income from the Thames Street property to the Company's general account. The 'Hall Fund' continued to accrue interest but the search for a hall was once again, quietly it seems, dropped.

Hard Times

The failure of the attempt to construct a hall ushered in a new malaise in the Company's affairs. The Company continued to function but its purpose seems to have been obscured. The importance of the Company was undermined by legislative changes to the franchise of the City of London. Members of the livery companies lost the exclusive right to vote in parliamentary elections in the City. The lack of a devoted meeting place was perhaps a cause of the problem. Either out of convenience or economy the Company took to meeting outside the City. For a time the Company was holding inquorate meetings at the *Trafalgar Hotel*, Greenwich, a fashionable if less than central hostelry noted for its whitebait dinners. The old problems of non-attendance surfaced again and by 1872 the Court, after four successive cancelled meetings, noted 'considerable inconvenience' of the absence of members and the 'great decrease' of new liverymen. The failure to find new liverymen was, according to the Committee deputised to investigate the problem seriously affecting the renewals that are so essential, of members of the Company by the introduction of young lives, and that by means of which only the capabilities of the Company to keep up its constituency under its charters can be preserved.

The Committee recommended that 'strenuous efforts be made by those engaged in the distillery business to add to the livery any additional members that can be obtained for it'. The problem continued and by 1874 a crisis point appears to have been reached. Membership of the Court of Assistants stood at 20 but the livery had dwindled to some 22 men. The Court of Assistants again set up a committee which examined some drastic measures such as seeking a new charter or private Act of Parliament, to cut the numbers required for a quorum of the Court of Assistants. As the numbers of the Court of Assistants was set by the Company's original charters, any change in its constitution neccessitated government approval. But the Committee went further, going so far as to contemplate effectively winding up the Company by amalgamating it with another livery company, 'there appearing to exist so many difficulties in obtaining a sufficient number of freemen or liverymen for keeping up the Company as an independent body or company'. In the event these extreme measures were not taken. The Committee recommended, with an air of barely-repressed desperation, that members of the Court of Assistants use 'their exertions and influence to resuscitate and reanimate the Company of Distillers so that it might be maintained and kept alive by the prestige of the trade for ages yet to come'. The Committee looked back to the renewal of the Company after the redemptions of 1826, when those who joined the Company were summonsed under the threat of a possible court action. But the reality of the situation seems to have prevailed when the Court of Assistants ordered the Clerk to 'abstain as closely as possible from using terms of a threatening character' when drafting a printed circular inviting members of the trade to take up the freedom. The only way for the Company to sustain itself was to appeal to the force of tradition rather than to real legal powers.

The attempt at renewal succeeded slowly in building up the membership. Twelve new freemen, three of them at least being connected with the distillery trade, joining the Company in the years between 1876 and 1879. This new intake was to be followed by up to a dozen new freemen being taken on in the 1880s and 1890s. Slowly the composition of the Company began to change yet again, as the direct link with the distilling industry became supplanted by men involved in a wide variety of businesses only tangential to the arts of Theodore de Mayerne. New members included stockbrokers, company secretaries, surveyors, architects, insurance underwriters and other typically late Victorian professions, but also not a few newer occupations. The grant of a freedom to an electrical engineer, a Percy Kingdom Wilson of 'Ethelstan', Waldegrave Road, Teddington in July 1894 is as good an example as any of the changing composition of the Company in this era of transition. But the link with the old trade was not completely abandoned. A core of the membership were commercial distillers, and individual distillers, such as Henry Jameson of the Jameson Distillery, Dublin, were invited to take up membership. But their numbers were augmented by a new generation of freemen whose association with the spirits trade was commercial rather than industrial. The Distillers had earlier enrolled freemen who were engaged in ancillary commercial trades such as importers and shippers of fortified wines. There numbers were to grow in years to come and were to do much to revive the old connection with the trade. In addition new connections were formed with the trade via charitable grants to new organisations such as the Wine and Spirits Benevolent Society and the Licensed Victuallers Asylum.

The Livery Companies Commission and Technical Education

The defensive response of the Distillers' Company to the renewal of attempts at reforming the institutions of the City of London was symptomatic of its weakness in the late 19th century. The Company had joined together with other companies in actively opposing the London Corporation Bill of 1852, which proposed to limit the political exclusivity of the livery company franchise, paying £10 to the fund collected by the Clerk of the Spectacle Makers' Company to lobby Parliament. In 1877 the Company contributed to the defeat of a further motion in the House of Commons which threatened to interfere in the powers of the livery companies. The appointment of the Royal Commission on the London Livery Companies in 1881 was the final, greatest challenge posed to livery companies by the municipal reformers. The Commission had wide powers to require information on the government and internal finances of the livery companies. The answer of the Company to the Commission's queries was baldly to refer to the return made to the 1833 Municipal Corporations Commission with the added statement that 'the real property of the company has increased in value since the date of the report and that the Company has become otherwise more wealthy'. The Livery Companies Commission chided the Company for its brevity, 'as the statement does no more than refer the Commissioners to a report which is nearly fifty years old', but it took no further action. At the same time the Court of Assistants took legal opinion as to the possibility of transferring the 'Hall Fund', now grown to over £4,000, to the Company's general account. The fall of the Liberal government in 1885 ended any immediate threat of legislation based on the findings of the Livery Companies Commission and thereafter the prospect of further interference receded.

One way in which the livery companies responded to the challenge of the reformers was to seek to promote technical education, attempting to re-invent the medieval rôle of guilds in training. The City and Guilds Institute, founded in 1877, was in part a response to criticism of the livery companies that they did little to help the people who actually worked in those trades. Though it was slow in getting off the ground, The City.and Guilds Institute gradually attracted wide support for its provision of a wide range of skills training. In October 1886 a senior member of the Court, E.L.Beckwith, told the Court that he intended to propose that the Company set up a perpetual scholarship at the City and Guilds Institute 'to advance technical education especially in reference to the Art or Mystery of Distilling'. Beckwith's proposal was initially voted down but in April

1889 he succeeded in persuading the Court to set up a prize worth £5 for a technological examination in spirit manufacture. The first exams were not a success as insufficient numbers of candidates presented themselves. Beckwith evidently hoped that the experiment would lead to a further contribution by the Company but he was evidently rebuffed and he left the Court of Assistants with a bitter letter of resignation. Despite this the Company's support for the prize continued for some years, but the grant was later rescinded. When the immediate threat of reform receded it would appear that the Company's interest in technical education waned.

The Distillers in the 20th Century

If in the late Victorian period the Company appears to have undergone a crisis of confidence, the new century was to be an era of rediscovery of some of the older foundations of the Company. The First World War was a time of retrenchment and increased charitable donations. Immediately after the outbreak of war the Court of Assistants at a special meeting 'to consider what steps should be taken, in view of the war crisis' voted to abandon its October livery dinner and to give 100 guineas to the National Relief Fund. In the second year of the War the Court left it to the Master and Wardens to use their discretion in deciding whether to go ahead with the October dinner, with misplaced optimism, 'if the war had not come to an end'. The War did not end and all traditional conviviality was suspended. The occupants of the Upper Thames Street property, wholesale ironmongers, were granted a reduction in rent because of the enlistment of a partner and the disruption caused by war and a strike in the building trade. Liverymen and members of the Court of Assistants took up the call to arms. The Court minutes for these years record letters of condolence to the families of those lost, congratulations to those who received decorations and, in one instance, a telegram sent to a member of the Court of Assistants, Warden J.L. Norris, at a rest camp at Port Said with the clipped tones of the era: 'best wishes, good luck. The Distillers Company'. When many of the serving members returned from war they were to have a distinct impact on the Company's identity. The inter-war Court of Assistants contained a leavening of officers and ex-officers.*

The gradual replenishment of the Company's membership by a steady trickle of new men of the Victorian and Edwardian period was followed by a rush of new members in the 1920s and '30s. With an air of efficiency perhaps brought on by the wartime experience of younger members of the Court of Assistants, the Company actively recruited from amongst the senior managers of the big distilleries and wine shipping and importing firms. The results were impressive: between 1919 and 1938, 43 new liverymen were taken on, most of them chairmen, managing directors or partners of distillers, breweries and wine shipping firms. This new intake included representatives from some of the most important firms, including familiar names in the Company's history such as Seagar, Evans and Co., as well as new ones such as the North British Distillery Co., John Dewar and Son, Ltd., Highland Distillers, Ltd., James Buchanan and Co., Fremlin Bros. Ltd., Mentzendorff Ltd. and Gonzalez y Byass Ltd. In addition men from ancillary industries joined, such as a representative of the Direct Supply Aerated Water Co., who became free in 1933. This new intake helped to breathe life into the Company's traditional bonds with the distilling industry. An interesting example of the renewed connections during the inter-war period is the support shown by the Company in 1923 for the South London Licensed Victuallers Trade Protection Association.

The Second World War's impact on the Company was no less dramatic. The Upper Thames Street property was partially damaged by bombing in November 1940 and the area around it was devastated in this and later raids. The Blitz paved the way for the comprehensive redevelopment of the metropolitan area and from October 1944 the Company was aware that the City's planners had earmarked the area around the site for road widening in a projected post-war redevelopment. From this point the Company began to contemplate the sale of the site. By now the buildings on the site were 115 years old and the Company's surveyors recommended sale of the site to the City Corporation. This was finally carried out in April 1961 for the sum of £10,000, a small amount in comparison to later

---

*   This may in part explain the financial support shown to the Organisation for the Maintenance of Supply in 1925, a voluntary body set up to maintain supplies and services in the event of industrial action. The O.M.S. was used to help break the General Strike a year later.

property values but one which, in the depressed state of the property market of the time, was perhaps the best the Company could hope for.

But if the war had thus destroyed a tangible legacy of the Company's past, in other ways the old links with the origins of the Distillers' Company were renewed and strengthened. The distilling industry was itself subject to many changes. Many of the mature family-run distilling firms of the 19th century disappeared or amalgamated as new large-scale distilleries, functioning as public companies, were established. It might be thought the social and economic trends of the 20th century would have rendered any residual connections with the modern distilling industry completely irrelevant. Certainly most if not all of the livery companies had long abandoned their old connections with the trades they once comprised. Yet, if anything in the case of the Distillers, the opposite is true.

The noticeable Hibernian air of the inter-war intake of new liverymen helped to forge new connections with the distilling trade. In October 1954 Sir Reginald Macdonald-Buchanan entrusted the Company with £2,500

3 March 1965, official adoption of the London Scottish Regiment.
The piper on the right is carrying a banner with the Company's coat of arms.

to fund a £350 scholarship 'in chemistry work applied to the whisky trade' in the form of a bursary to be established at Imperial College, University of London. The Company consulted with the directors of the Distillers Company Ltd. in attempting to set up the scheme. Due to lack of progress in setting up the scholarship, a short-term policy of using the interest arising out of the fund 'to pay for one or two selected young men in the wine trade to attend at various distilleries in Scotland to learn something of the distilling trade' was set up. As with earlier attempts at promoting technical training, this experiment did not prove entirely successful though the Macdonald-Buchanan bursaries were granted for a number of years. The Macdonald-Buchanan gift formed the nucleus of the Company's charitable undertakings in more recent years. Further ties with Scotland were formed in this period through the adoption of units of the armed forces. The decision by the Company to adopt the London Scottish Regiment in 1965 confirmed this new association with Scottish distillers, the Court noting how 'any Scottish organisation would have a distinct affinity with the Distillers Company'. With the Regiment's permission, pipers from the London Scottish have become a regular feature of the loving cup ceremony at the annual Livery and Ladies' Banquet held at the Mansion House. Since 1994 the symbolic link with Scotland has been reinforced by the adoption of the Type 23 Frigate H.M.S. *Montrose*.

The recent past has seen a further extension of the renewed affinities of the Company with the distilling, wine and spirits industry. The grant of the honorary livery to the High Commissioner for Canada, a Company tradition initiated in 1959, gave recognition to the importance of the North American industry in the import trade and the historical closeness of the Canadian and Scottish distilleries. A similar grant of honorary membership has been given to the Portuguese Ambassador in recognition of the association between London-based port shippers and that country's most famous liquid commodity. More recently the Company has formed new informal bonds with the Scottish distilling industry through the Keepers of the Quaich, an organisation formed to promote the fame of Scotch whisky throughout the world.

H.M.S. *MONTROSE*

Type 23 Frigate.

The latest class to enter service with the Royal Navy in 1994; the Company 'adopted' the ship during the same year.

The rôle of the Company today has been to maintain the traditions of its history by strengthening the association with the distilling industry and by taking part in the many activities associated with the collective life of the City of London and the livery companies. These activities include assistance to various charities and other organisations. The Company contributes regularly to the Wine and Spirit Trades' Benevolent Society, the principal charity for the trade, and many Past Masters have acted as chairmen to 'the Benevolent'. The Company also regularly makes donations to the annual Lord Mayor's Appeal and a number of other charities. In the field of education the Company annually provides a scholarship through the Wine and Spirits Education Trust to cover the costs of study visits to United Kingdom distilleries. Candidates are selected from amongst those receiving outstanding marks in the diploma paper examined by the Trust. In addition the Company nominates one trustee to the Trust's governing body.

The search for a hall, a concern of the Company since its inception, has been given new impetus by the opportunities provided by the availability of redundant churches in the City of London. It is hoped that through the founding of a hall the associations with the distilling industry will be given a more tangible basis, and provide a meeting place, both for the Distillers' Company as well as for the industry as a whole. The final outcome of these endeavours remains to be seen but, as this history has attempted to show, this three-and-a-half century long tradition, not without its gaps and lapses, forms the most striking theme of the Company's history. The renewal over the centuries of the Company's links with the trade in various forms has repeatedly reinvigorated the Company and infused it with renewed purpose. It is remarkable that this venerable tradition of the Company's history has lost none of its potency and it remains the essence of the Company. It is this that makes the Distillers unique today.

To this day the link with the trade has been reinforced. Between sixty and seventy per cent of the present liverymen are either directly involved in distilling, or the wine trade and associated trades such as cork merchants, bottle manufacturers and label producers and specialists in shipping for the wine and spirits industry. The Company's yearly round of luncheons and dinners, to which members of the trade are regularly invited, provides an atmosphere of conviviality and informality in which those involved in the multifarious branches of the industry can meet. The Company thus in a very real sense fulfills an original purpose of its founders, though the concept of 'networking' may have been somewhat alien to the likes of Sir Theodore de Mayerne. So long as these bonds with the industry are cherished and maintained the Company can face the future with a renewed sense of purpose.

Appendix I
Masters of the Worshipful Company of Distillers since 1638

(Gaps indicate where this information is unavailable)

1638	Sir Thomas Cademan		1705	Thomas Wickham
1663	Ralph Triplett		1714	William Diston
1664	Francis Heath		1715	Joseph Wight
1665	Francis Heath		1716	Jonathan Boulter
1666	Robert Terrey		1717	Israel Wilkes
1667	Robert Terrey		1718	Anthony Holbeche
1668	Thomas Whittle		1719	William Estwicke
1669	Gervase Rosser		1720	Francis Stonnard
1670	Robert Taylor		1721	Thomas Browne
1674	Thomas Rawlinson		1722	Jonathan Fuller
1675	Gervase Seaton		1723	William Jarman
1676	Joseph Harrison		1724	Percival Hobson
1677	James Woods		1725	Edward Bulpen
1678	George Clark		1726	William Gardner
1679	Thomas Edwards		1727	James Clarke
1680	Daniel Wight		1728	Sisson Roberts
1681	John Heath		1708	Samuel Palmer
1682	John Elwick		1729	George Wingfield
1683	John Vyner		1730	Stonyer Plaisted
			1731	John Wilkes
1693	Edward Roberts		1732	Valentine Brewis
1694	William Barnes		1733	Sampson Fenn
1695	Thomas Henning		1734	Robert Barnard
1696	William Jerman		1735	George Baker
1697	Thomas Plaisted		1736	Thomas Maynard
1698	Thomas Mackley		1737	Richard Farrington
1699	John East		1738	Edmund Bathurst
1700	Joseph How		1739	Thomas Tomes
1701	John Hyett		1740	Richard Lawrence
1702	John Hawkins		1741	Richard Grove
1703	Samuel Robinson		1742	Thomas Cooke
1704	Samuel Barker		1743	John Barnett

1744	Daniel Terrett		1788	Samuel Liptrap
1745	Jonathan Hall		1789	Marmaduke Langdale
1746	Henry Saunders		1790	Richard Smart
1747	William Farman		1791	Thomas Chance
1748	John Turnpenny		1792	George Acton
1749	Lodowick Mansfield		1793	John Wollaston
1750	John Lloyd		1794	Richard Hopkins
1751	Richard Benson		1795	Thomas Langdale
1752	William Cornish		1796	Marmaduke Langadale
1753	George Jenyns		1797	William Fowler Jones
1754	Richard Blunt		1798	William Fowler Jones
1755	Calvert Bann		1799	Mark Hodgson
1756	Simon Fuller Wilkes		1800	John Hughes
1757	John Shewell		1801	Robert Rodgers
1758	Thomas Roddy		1802	Joseph Benwell
1759	John Bindley		1803	John Liptrap
1760	William Jellicoe		1804	John Reid
1761	Vincent Legatt		1805	Valentine Cooke
1762	Francis Magnus		1806	William Sayer
1763	Mark Bell		1807	John Bockett
1764	William Rogers		1808	Russell Skinner
1765	Edmond Woods		1809	Joseph Skinner
1766	Isaac Kemp		1810	Alexander Gordon
1767	Robert Walsham		1811	William Knight
1768	Wilkshear West		1812	George Scholey
1769	John Ewart		1813	George Scholey
1770	Thomas Winspear		1814	Laurence Shirley
1771	John Jones		1815	Samuel Liptrap
1772	Thomas Baker		1816	James Drage
1773	Groves Wheeler		1817	Henry Weymouth
1774	Joseph Hales		1818	James Chapple
1775	Cornelius Van Mildert		1819	James Langdale
1776	William Brackstone		1820	Thomas Davis
1777	John Cooke		1821	Francis Tunstall
1778	Richard Belson		1822	Marmaduke Langdale
1779	John Guy		1823	Francis Worthington
1780	Joseph Skinner		1824	John Hughes
1781	Robert Territt		1825	William Fowler Jones
1782	John Rex		1826	Thomas Atkinson
1783	Christopher Woodham		1827	George Watson
1784	Anthony Facer Kemp		1828	Andrew Mackenzie
1785	John Woodham		1829	Edward Bowerbank
1786	George Hodgson		1830	John Bowerbank
1787	Thomas Sayer		1831	John Chapple

1832	John Roberts	1876	F. Seager Hunt
1833	William Knight	1877	Richard Wilson
1834	Samuel Richards	1878	James Story
1835	Joseph Vickers	1879	James Vallentin
1836	James Goldie	1880	William Emery
1837	Ealand Adler	1881	John Meek
1838	William Evans	1882	Edward Vickers
1839	John Vickers	1883	Grimble Vallentin
1840	Noah Slee	1884	Walter Goldsmith
1841	W.S. Browning	1885	Edward Bowley
1842	Samuel Burn	1886	Charles Fox
1843	J.A.T. Smyth	1887	Thomas Fox
1844	John Nicholson	1888	Benjamin Parker
1845	William Jackson	1889	Charles Fox
1846	James Lys Seager	1890	Frederick Capron
1847	John Johnson	1891	Frederick Imbert-Terry
1848	James Scott Smith	1892	Charles Gordon
1849	Joseph Claypole	1893	Grimble Vallentin
1850	William Nicholson	1894	Watson Osmond
1851	George Smith	1895	Harry Newman
1852	John Vickers	1896	Thomas Courtenay
1853	William Goldsmith	1897	John Fleuret
1854	Thomas Fox	1898	Robert Cooper
1855	Charles Curtis	1900-1	W.G.F. Whittingstall
1856	John A.F. Bennett	1901-2	E.A. Baylis
1857	Edward Vickers	1902-3	C.H. Shoppee
1858	Duncan Menzies	1903-4	F. Brooks Page
1859	Frederick Capron	1904-5	A.J. Norris
1860	Joseph Boord	1905-6	D. Malcolm Scott
1861	John Nicholson	1906-7	Grimble Vallentin
1862	William Gray Jackson	1907-8	W.A. Carden
1863	William Nicholson	1908-9	R.E. Cunningham
1864	William Foster White	1909-10	Harry J. Newman
1865	Christopher Wilson	1910-11	Col. W. Nicholls VD
1866	John A.T. Smyth	1911-12	B.M. Parker
1867	James Hunt	1912-13	F.W. Imbert-Terry
1868	Charles Gordon	1913-14	Robert Cooper
1869	James Vallentin	1914-15	D. Malcolm Scott
1870	George Orme	1915-16	D. Malcolm Scott
1871	Edward Beckwith	1916	A.J. Norris
1872	Thomas Fox	1917	James Vallentin
1873	John Burnett	1917-18	John Marks
1874	Thomas Boord	1918-19	A.F.A. Imbert-Terry MBE
1875	John Henry Gent	1919-20	Harry J. Newman

1920-21	D. Malcolm Scott	1960-61	Thomas Kingsley Collett
1921-22	Lt. Col. Sir Geo.A.E. Hussey JP	1961-62	Harold Stanley Redding
1922-23	Major E.P. Nicolls DSO TD	1962-63	Victor Leslie Seyd
1923-24	Charles E.J. Cary-Elwes	1963-64	Albert Rouyer Guillet
1924-25	Thomas P. Dorman	1964-65	Sir William Steward
1925-26	George Haslett	1965-66	Brig. Alexander Douglas McKechnie DSO OBE TD
1926-27	John Joseph Hunt JP		
1927-28	Arthur W. Folks	1966-67	Major Guy Lionel Greville Harry TD
1928-29	F.W. Imbert-Terry		
1929-30	Harry J. Newman JP	1967-68	John Percival Finney
1930-31	E. Price Hallowes	1968-69	The Hon. Frederick Francis George Hennessy MBE
1931-32	Thomas George Vickery		
1932-33	Captain Reginald Corfield	1969-70	Arthur Philip Casey Lyons
1933-34	Charles Edwards JP	1970-71	Randolph Wemyss Dunsire
1934-35	Reginald Hunt	1971-72	William Emile Rouyer Guillet
1935-36	Brig. Gen. Charles S. Davidson CB	1972-73	Alan Seymour Lamboll JP
1936-37	Major R.W. Cooper OBE MC JP	1973-74	Guiseppe Umberto Salvi OBE
1937-38	Sidney A. Newton	1974-75	John Henry William Dunbar
1938-39	John A. Dewar	1975-76	Col. Geoffrey Vardon Churton MBE MC TD DL
1939-40	John A. Dewar		
1940-41	John A. Dewar	1976-77	Peter Bartholomew Reynier MC
1941-42	John A. Dewar	1977-78	Geoffrey Ernest Nobes
1942-43	R. William Byass	1978-79	Peter Hasslacher
1943-44	A.F.A. Imbert-Terry MBE	1979-80	George Potts
1944-45	Lt. Col. Sir Geo.A.E. Hussey JP	1980-81	Walter Sichel
1945-46	Charles E.J. Cary-Elwes	1981-82	William Ian Baverstock Brooks
1946-47	E. Price Hallowes	1982-83	Michael Boileau Henderson
1947-48	Major E.P. Nicholls DSO TD	1983-84	Patrick Robert Henry Lynch
1948-49	Major Victor H. Seyd	1984-85	David Robert Lamdin
1949-50	Sir Reginald Spence	1985-86	Thomas Norman Ritchie TD
1950-51	Alexander John Buckley Rutherford CVO CBE	1986-87	Frank Charles Minoprio
		1987-88	Alan Burrough CBE
1951-52	Alexander John Buckley Rutherford CVO CBE	1988-89	Norman Cary Burrough CBE
		1989-90	Alexander James MacDonald-Buchanan
1952-53	Major R. MacDonald-Buchanan CVO MBE MC DL		
		1990-91	John Michael Broadbent
1953-54	Sydney Frederick John Fells	1991-92	Vincent Larvan
1954-55	William Charlton Edwards	1992-93	Nigel Causton Strofton
1955-56	Ronald Hughes	1993-94	S.W. Morrison
1956-57	Edward Herbert Clark	1994-95	Michael Druitt
1957-58	Lt. Col. Alexander Malcolm Scott	1995-96	Dr. Peter Hallgarten
1958-59	Alcide William Henry Le Forestier	1996-97	Anthony Charlton Edwards
1959-60	Frederick Armine Cockburn		

Appendix II
Clerks to the Worshipful Company of Distillers since 1638

(With year of election)

1638	John Carwytham
1668	John Green
1698	John Green
1721	Thomas Honeywood
1724	Thomas Hardwick
1773	William Clavill
1779	Bury Hutchinson
1824	Bury Hutchinson, jr.
1835	Thomas Browning
1882	E.A. Baylis
1898	T.G. Vickery
1931	F.G. Earle
1940	H.J. Edwards
1944	George Harris
1955	H.B. Dehn
1991	Christopher Hughes

Appendix III
Lord Mayors of London who were members of the Worshipful Company of Distillers

1812	George Scholey
1845	John Johnson

Bibliography and Further Reading

The early and later history of the science of distillation is discussed in:

R.J. Forbes, *A Short History of the Art of Distillation* (Leiden, E.J.Brill, 1948)

For the early history of distilling in England see:

C.A.Wilson, 'burnt wines and cordial waters: the early history of distilling' *Folk Life*, xiii (1979)

J.Thirsk, *Economic Policy and Projects* (1969)

Theodore de Mayerne's contribution to medical practice is discussed in:

Allen G. Debus, *The English Paracelsians* (1965)

For the struggle over incorporation of the Distillers, and the rôle of the Apothecaries and the Corporation see:

Robert Ashton, *The City and the Court, 1603-1643*

Charles Webster, *The Great Instauration: Science and Reform in Seventeenth Century England* (1970)

The history of the distilling industry in the seventeenth and eighteenth centuries, and the public controversies surrounding it, are discussed in:

D.M. George, *London Life in the Eighteenth Century* (1925)

Peter Earle, *The Making of the English Middle Class: Business, Society and Family Life in London* (1989)

Peter Clarke, *The English Alehouse: a Social History 1200-1830* (1986)

Peter Clarke, 'The Mother Gin Controversy in the Early Eighteenth Century', *Transactions of the Royal Historical Society* (1987)

George Rudé, '"Mother Gin" and the London Riots of 1736', in *Paris and London in the Eighteenth Century* (1970), pp.201-21

Index